A Pocket-Sized Jumble of Writing Prompts

By Tyrean Martinson

Paperback Edition

Second Edition

With Wings of Light Publishing

First Edition 2014

With Wings of Light Publishing

PRAISE FOR A POCKET-SIZED JUMBLE OF WRITING PROMPTS

"This is the perfect book for somebody who enjoys writing from prompts.

I've already used some of these prompts during the creation of my 2015 A to Z Challenge flash fiction pieces, as well as my haiku writing.

Prompts never fail to get my creative juices flowing so I know that I'll make continued use of this nifty resource." Michelle Wallace

"Wonderful little book of story prompts. It would be great for bloggers, seasoned writers, or for those who would like to dabble in writing and don't know where to start." – Elizabeth Seckman

"These prompts helped me sink deeper into my writing. They are a good way to "prime the pump" to get started. You can take the digital book with you anywhere on your phone and squeeze in some writing time every day." – Carla F.

"The prompts are brief snapshots into a creative journey. I've only had the book a couple of days and already the juices are

flowing... 3 poems, 2 short stories and a million ideas fluttering through my mind. I recommend this to anyone who either needs a jump-start or who enjoys writing from prompts." - Ravyne

"Need ideas. Get them here." - Diana Wilder

Forward for the Second Edition

For several years, this book was my bread-and-butter book. If no other books were selling, this one was. I didn't know why, but it seemed to find an audience. A local bookstore sold more copies of this book than any of my fiction books. A local adult group of writers used it, then a local group of teen writers used it. A group of writers I didn't know used it in a different state, then someone used it in a different country. I was amazed by the use it received and the people who loved it.

As we entered into March of 2020 and life as we knew it came to a screeching halt for COVID-19, and disasters piled upon disasters, I sank into a month of journal writing. I struggled. I went back to writing prompt books and rediscovered my love of words. Taking a look at the first edition of this book, I decided it needed a fresh cover and some new extras.

I created this second edition for those who haven't seen it yet, in the hopes that the added bits of writing tips can help more writers find a creative and fresh start to their regular writing practice.

Creativity can help us find light in these dark times. Write. Imagine. Hope. And start again.

Original Introduction

As a writer, I have discovered that I like a particular kind of writing prompt, the simplest of writing prompts. The books that give entire scenarios or seasonal order don't tempt me at all because I want the freedom to imagine.

A simple word or phrase on a blank sheet of paper gathers momentum as I wonder at what it could mean, where it could take place, why, and what if? What if the words "green turtle" aren't referring to a turtle at all? What if it's the shield formation for a group of space pirates? What if? And then, I write.

Another time with that same simple prompt, I might ask: who does this turtle belong to? Has it escaped? who finds it? And then, I write.

So, this book contains over 500 simple writing prompts, all jumbled out of order so that each may stand alone to evoke a new story, a new poem, or a new reflection. Many artists I know also like to draw or doodle and these prompts could work as drawing prompts, as well as writing prompts.

Write, reflect, imagine, and enjoy!

Original Note on Using Writing Prompts

Writing prompts can start a writer or artist in a variety of ways. As I mentioned in the introduction, a prompt can be a starting place to a story, a poem, a reflection, or a drawing.

A writer can ask themselves "what, where, when, how, why, or who" questions before starting to write.

Or, a writer can set a timer, open a page, and write as fast as possible on the topic that first comes to mind.

These prompts can start a daily writing practice, a weekly writing practice, or a study of words on paper over a lengthier time.

A writer with a story already in progress could use these prompts to delve deeper into their characters. Again, this requires asking questions like: what would my main character do with agree turtle? why would my character remember things lost? what kind of explosion would actually make my character jump?

A poet, when using these prompts, could use each prompts as the starting line of a poem, or as an image to start a poem.

A reflective journalist may use these prompts to write about the world around them, as a jumping off point for random thoughts or planned reflections.

A writer can use these prompts with pen and paper, or with a touch screen.

Each writer can approach this book in the way that suits his/her writing best.

Happy Writing!

FIRST 50 PROMPTS

the moment that defines awkwardness

walk the red carpet

watch for me by moonlight

"do not go gentle into that good night"
(Dylan)

the moment before the alarm goes off

cliffs of despair

call of the wild

What's in a name?

marshmallows melting in hot cocoa

ocean swells

holy socks

in the wide, waiting land

wishing the earth would swallow me up

"to waken this long-cherished morn"
(Tonna)

driving rain

moss-grown trees

common as mud

a sail on the horizon

at the snap

grabbing each branch for the climb

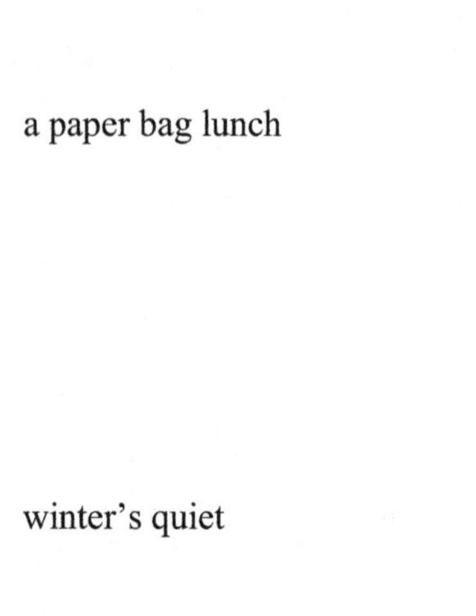

a paper bag lunch

winter's quiet

dear angry henchmen,

the doors of the sun closed

"When the hour is hushed" (David)

purple crocus spring

leave the trenches

a furtive glance

between attic and basement

dancing in the rain

an evergreen forest reaching up to an
overpass

on the train

a dark shadow on the ocean wave behind her

a deer nibbles apples left to rot in the grass

shallow thoughts

temperatures vary

straddling the border

torpedo lights

running in the rhythm of the dark

tail-wagging happiness

thin ice

forgiving and forgetting

geometry poetry

to have and to hold

a recipe for cherry turnovers

a first-place ribbon

a snoring dog

folding a map

back in black

closing a door

Make Everything Searchable

Whether a writer keeps a series of paper journals, or dictates their work into a recording app, or writes in a series of word documents, a writer's life is made much easier when simple organizational tools are used to make everything searchable.

In a word document or recording app program, this involves naming the individual documents clearly and sorting them into folders based on type, genre, and/or year.

In paper journals, a writer can create the same or similar level of organization by creating a table of contents in the first few pages (or the last few pages) of a journal, numbering the pages, and titling each entry with subject names and dates. While numbering the pages in a journal may seem like a mind-numbing exercise, it can be done while the writer is writing each entry.

The Table of Contents takes up a few pages at the beginning (or end) of a journal and needs only a title for each entry and a page number for each entry. I often include a date for each entry in the Table of Contents as well, because sometimes I am writing about similar subjects in other contexts and places outside of my journal.

These simple, quick tools can save writers hours of frustration and grief, making every poem, story, or idea searchable in a document folder on a PC or in the Table of Contents in a journal.

A writer could even take this a step further and keep journals according to date on a bookshelf or in a bin.

In any case, it's something I recommend as a writer. Floating word documents without much for a title or journal entries with no page numbers or entry names frustrated me for many years. It's true that I can't always think of a good title. If I struggle with it, then I title it by the name of the character that's in the work, the place of the setting, or the type of writing it is along with the date.

Something that is a must for the sanity of a writer is having a backup file for any word documents. A writer can create a backup with an external drive or by sending a draft of the work to themselves via e-mail. Cloud storage can also help, but not all writers feel it is secure enough. It's up the writer. These tools can help. Try one or all of them. See what works for you.

PROMPTS 51-100

periodic table game

corn fields in all directions

stepping on a scorpion

not seeing the possibilities

the day after the funeral

teddy bear tea time

skydiving

tea whistling

a damsel not in distress

ground cinnamon sprinkled over sugared
toast

tater tots for lunch

a field of butterflies

the worst commencement speech

an uncomfortable relative

stepping stones

origami cranes made from birthday
wrapping

an unexpected switch in the dark

a deck warmed by sunshine

stale bread and sour milk

left-handed scissors

a drop in the bucket

the forever love

a black hole

house of cards

the greatest challenge

Angels We Have Heard

we didn’t start the fire

under the raging sun

waves gently lapping at the shore

the train to nowhere

a father's love

a cup of joe

for you and I are past our dancing days
(Shakespeare)

fields of green clover

scars

funny business

diamonds winking on her finger

in the shape of this night (Patchen)

in the mirror darkly

a game well-played

a chain is only as good as its weakest link

a moment of hesitation

a letter to a younger me

a man without a face

the forever war

event horizon

let them eat cake

in a pickle

dust up

under the desk

Writing Space and Mindset

Where do you write?

Is it important to have a particular space, like a writing desk tucked away into a special office room or corner of your house? Do you need to have just the right kind of composition book or laptop?

While many studies have been done on how to create new and healthy habits using a particular space in your environment to help you get into the right mindset, I think you can write anywhere, any time.

Mindset matters most.

I love writing anywhere - my car, on my couch, in a “special chair” in my house, in bed, at the dining room table, at my desk, in coffee shops, in dance studio lobbies (when my daughters danced), waiting rooms, and even at kayak races. I've written at home and abroad, on airplanes, trains, and buses. I’ve written with music, ambient noise, and silence only broken by the sound of my dog's feet on the hard floor.

What's my secret for doing this?

Mindset.

I am a writer; therefore, I write. I am a writer. This means I can write anywhere. I will write anywhere. I love writing.

It's true that there are days when doubt and insecurity eat at my writing mindset. The best way for me to beat that doubt and insecurity is to tell it off and to repeat my mantra from above: I am a writer; therefore, I write. I am a writer. This means I can write anywhere. I will write anywhere. I love writing.

It's sounds simple, but it requires self-discipline. I carry a notebook or journal with me wherever I go. I have an app downloaded on my phone for notes and google docs. I never leave home without a writing surface – journal, laptop, or phone. I give myself permission to write every day.

Give yourself permission to write. Write your own mantra. Repeat it. You can write. You are a writer. You can write anywhere. You can write any time.

You can use this for any type of writing or creative pursuit. Write your own affirmations to help you in your creative pursuits.

PROMPTS 101-150

a camera's eye view

an unlikely skeleton in the closet

dust the cares from the soles of your shoes

sacrifice

the favorite teacher

a foot in the door

interruptions

a sorry sight

food from the rescue mission

a moth fluttering against a bright window

below the belt

riding on the bus

taps played on the trombone

white glue and tissue paper stuck to my fingers

bell, book, and candle

fly on the wall

thundering waterfalls

a burly old raccoon bustles across the path

paddles flashing with sunlit water drops

bullies on the prowl

in like Flynn

a bolt from the blue

a horse, a horse, a kingdom for a horse

too tired to sleep

red sky at night, sailor's delight

all the world's a stage and we are merely
players

a jack o'lantern grin

gravity

things carried

curling up in a quilt of comfort

mystery meat dinner

a puddle of puppies

cut the mustard

ivory tower

jack of all trades

cracks in the sidewalk

a floating restaurant

blank space

barefoot in the rain

the final frontier

lighthouse

prodigal son/daughter

still waters run deep

things are not always what they seem

things remembered

light in the darkness

a cold corner

creepy shelf elves

living on a shoe string

about face

Five Reasons to Write Short Stories

You may be using these prompts to write essays, poetry, songs, or scripts. You may be using them as art prompts. If you have an interest in pursuing the craft of fiction writing in any length, here are five reasons to consider short stories.

1. Creativity Boost. Let's say you're stuck in the middle of your novel and you feel frustrated. A short story with a completely different cast of characters can free up your imagination so when you return to your novel, you have some imagination coursing through your veins.

2. Courage. If you submit those short stories, the process of submission can help you build up the courage you might need to self-publish or send query letters for your novel later.

3. Experience. When you get a short story published, you might go through an editing process with an editor first, or you might just get the elation of getting published.

4. A Sense of Accomplishment. Writing a short story should only take an hour to a month of your writing time. It's nice to have something get completed quickly. It gives a writer a sense of accomplishment. Story started, story done, and so on.

5. Word Choice. Working within a short word count forces a writer to pay attention to the vibrancy of each individual word. With a lot of short story practice, this skill starts to show in our novel writing.

PROMPTS 151-200

on the warpath

a dandelion woman

a round sorrow

a boat taxi

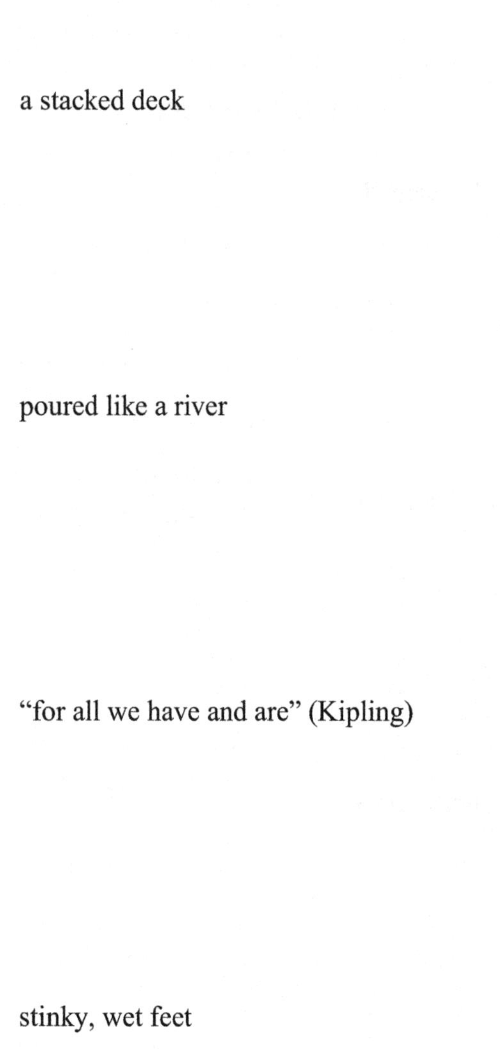

a stacked deck

poured like a river

“for all we have and are” (Kipling)

stinky, wet feet

boots too big to fill

divided lines

a wild rumpus at the library

a lean, stray cat slinking across the street

the bounds of modesty

apple pie a la mode melting on a plate

two angry men

an old key found in the dirt

a mother's love

laughter is the best medicine

we three kings

too awake to sleep

crunching leaves underfoot

out of the tawny sunset

java, sweet and hot

drag her on and make her laugh

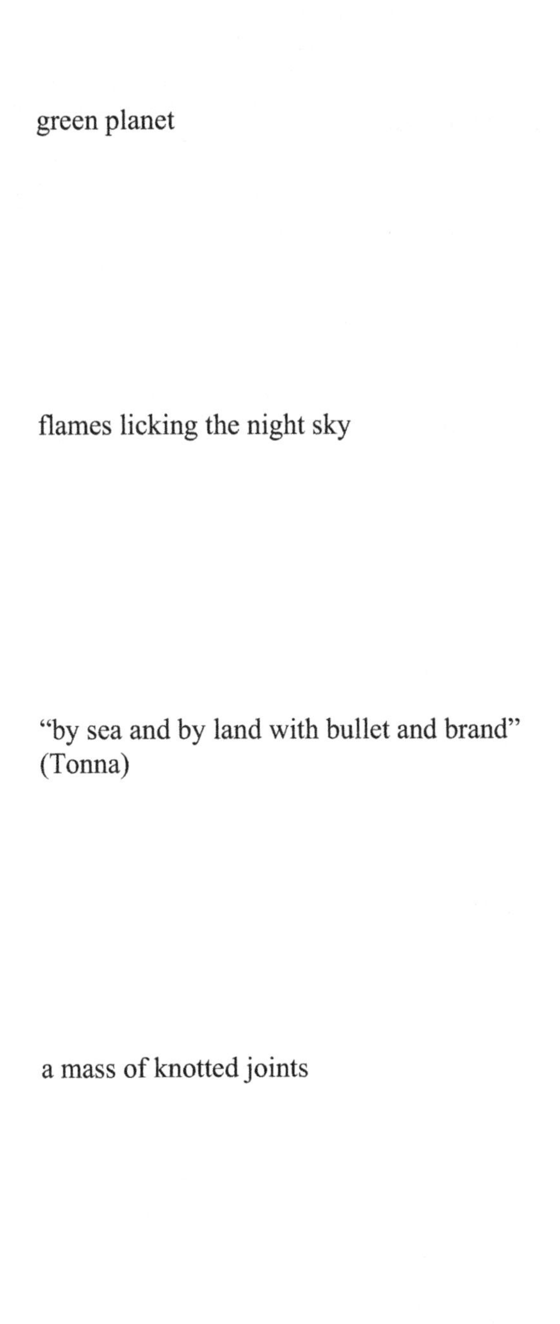

green planet

flames licking the night sky

“by sea and by land with bullet and brand”
(Tonna)

a mass of knotted joints

a muddy pond

grasshoppers on grassy hills

"the poetry of earth is ceasing never"
(Keats)

breathless

always fourth place

diving deep

pitching a tent in the snow

a forgotten hero

an art teacher with attitude

castles in the air

waiting in a doctor’s office

bread of life

burn the candle at both ends

an ill wind

a shiver of fear

a woman with a limp

wading in an ice-cold stream

a time capsule

the storytellers

the steady beat of rain on the roof

united we stand, divided we fall

the first step is always the hardest

More Ways to Use Writing Prompts

Read two to five prompts, mix them around, and write with all of them.

Read the prompt, set a timer for ten to twenty-five minutes, and write for the appointed time.

Choose a prompt and start telling a story out loud to your family or friends. Use talk-to-text to capture your story.

Choose three to five prompts, turn them into clues, and write a mystery story.

Choose three to five prompts and write about characters who embody those prompts.

Choose three to five prompts and write about settings which embody those prompts.

Choose a prompt and write a scene with only dialogue.

Choose a prompt and write a scene using all five senses, but no words.

Choose a prompt and create a work of art with it as your starting point: painting, drawing, collage, dance, music, etc.

Choose a prompt and write a song about it.

Choose a prompt and write a list of ideas from it. Then, choose one of those ideas, and write about it.

Create a new board game based on the prompt.

Draw a picture based on the prompt, then write about it.

With two or more people, have each person choose a prompt, draw a picture based on the prompt chosen, then pass the drawings to each other and write stories based on each other's drawings. (You can draw stick figures and write about each other's stick figure scenes.)

PROMPTS 201-250

no shrinking violet

moveable feast

bicycle marathon

a partner for life

deer tracks in the garden

a paper bag Christmas

bright leaves flying

a talent show

a drum march

landmines in the hallway

alike as two peas in a pod

one for the road

a letter from a long lost relative

dead men tell no tales

galaxies unlimited

making mud pies

a leveled playing field

silver linings

a narrow boat

the first time I saw her/him

old hat

back to life

a city girl

things forgotten

to love and to lose

holding hands

back to reality

sparkling snow

a compass rose

slipping in the mud

as mad as a hatter

behind the eight ball

ends of the earth

opinions in disguise

as different as chalk and cheese

April Fool

sunglasses at night

old vinyl records

sitting on the old, sagging porch

tower of strength

truth will out

the trees are listening

revenge is a dish best served cold

love is an anchor

an earthquake rumble

arts and crafts

snow falling on evergreens

a foolish knight

fields of waving grain

70 miles in the wilderness

THE SECRET OF WRITING SUCCESS

The secret of writing success is an overlooked reality.

Writing takes time, tenacity, and courage.

I've met talented writers who have never published or been published.

Why?

They don't send anything out.

No publisher is going to show up at your door demanding your brilliant work if no one knows you write.

Write. Finish. Send it.

Even if you give up for a while, you can pick up your pen again. Write. Finish. Send. Repeat.

Even if you struggle with health issues, family stuff, and life, you can pick up your pen again. Write. Finish. Send it. Repeat.

Do not wait to hear back from an editor, an agent, or a publisher before you begin to write your next project. Just keep writing.

Write. Finish. Send it. Repeat.

PROMPTS 251-300

don't rock the boat

a broken plate

burning the midnight oil

a princess kitchen

cut to the chase

a tree fort

exploration of the human heart

music to my ears

by the skin of your teeth

a secret society

a little red dress at a second hand store

dominos

a flying restaurant

something borrowed

adopted

dressed to the nines

an explosion

a prophecy kept secret

an explosion

singing in harmony without notes

as thick as thieves

trying on hats

wind-up toys on the run

all things must pass

shopping at the food bank

shimmering moonlit waves

clutter

a heavy responsibility

better late than never

an unorthodox alarm clock

leaving on a jet plane

oil, earth, and water

two to tango

opportunity knocks twice

the next step

wind whipping in her hair

a double-bladed kayak paddle

graduation

spilt milk

love conquers

quiet rebellion just in time

a censored movie

building foundations

spontaneous combustion

a charmed life

crocodile tears

far from a madding crowd

an alto’s solo

fellowship of friends

a closed door

WHY DO WE WRITE?

I've answered this question many times, and every time the answer varies slightly. I think it's a good question to revisit at least once a year for every writer. It's good to know the purpose behind our writing. What do we write for? Why do we do it? Once you know, print this out, or tuck it into a special place to revisit. Either post it on your wall as a daily inspiration or check it to see if it still rings true.

To give you a sense of what I mean by it changing slightly, I'll share two different ways I've answered this question.

A few years ago, I answered by saying:

When I was small, my grandmother told me stories from her childhood, and mixed in some fairy tales. My parents read to me and told me stories. I wanted to tell stories but struggled with getting the words out in the right order.

My first short story I remember feeling good about included a top hat that sang and danced (3rd grade).

In sixth grade, a teacher asked me if I wanted to be an author during a creative writing unit. She encouraged me to keep writing and working at my skill. In seventh, eighth, ninth, and tenth grades, I had teachers who encouraged me to write and grow into my potential as a would-be author. The trend continued in college. And yet, I still doubted. All the time. (More on that in a moment.)

The earliest story worlds which amazed me as a child included: Peter Pan's Neverland, Star Wars, fairy tales and folk tales, the Bible, Middle Earth, and Narnia. I wanted to write stories like those. I still do.

I love to write. It's bone deep, built into my soul, my memories, my DNA - a combination of nature and nurture.

Recently, I wrote this about why I specifically write fantasy:

I write fantasy for those who need/want the wild wonder, relaxing refuge, and inspiring imagination found in books where evil can be vanquished by a bar of chocolate or the roar of a lion.

In a way, the idea behind my writing hasn't changed, but I've refined it and shortened it into a statement I can post on my wall or on a social media page.

Reflect on this question. Why do you write? More specifically, why do you write your chosen genre(s)?

Knowing your "why" will help you immensely with the daily challenge of getting words on the page.

POMPTS 301-350

opening a window

instructions for life

skipping stones

cat’s cradle

fly by the seat of one's pants

a wet bed of yellow leaves

work that is real

sweet smiles

planting seeds in rich soil

extraordinary depths

shallow rivers

things that were lost

swimming to the buoy

head over heels

things found

a bowl of cherries

what the cat dragged in

we climb the cliffs to dive deep

sandstone terraces with burnt orange
archways

a door to another world

necessity is the mother of invention

on the bright side

a snow-crunching walk

under a midnight sun

blackberry jam bubbling to a boil

gangs at recess

a pinch of pixie dust

a green sea

starry night

patterns traced on paper

floundering in the mud

in the ocean deep

the alarm goes off

soar on wings like eagles

lullaby time

what’s done is done

“as merry as the day is long” (Shakespeare)

a soft-multicolored scarf around her waist

steeped tea

the tu-woo of an owl in the dark of early
morning

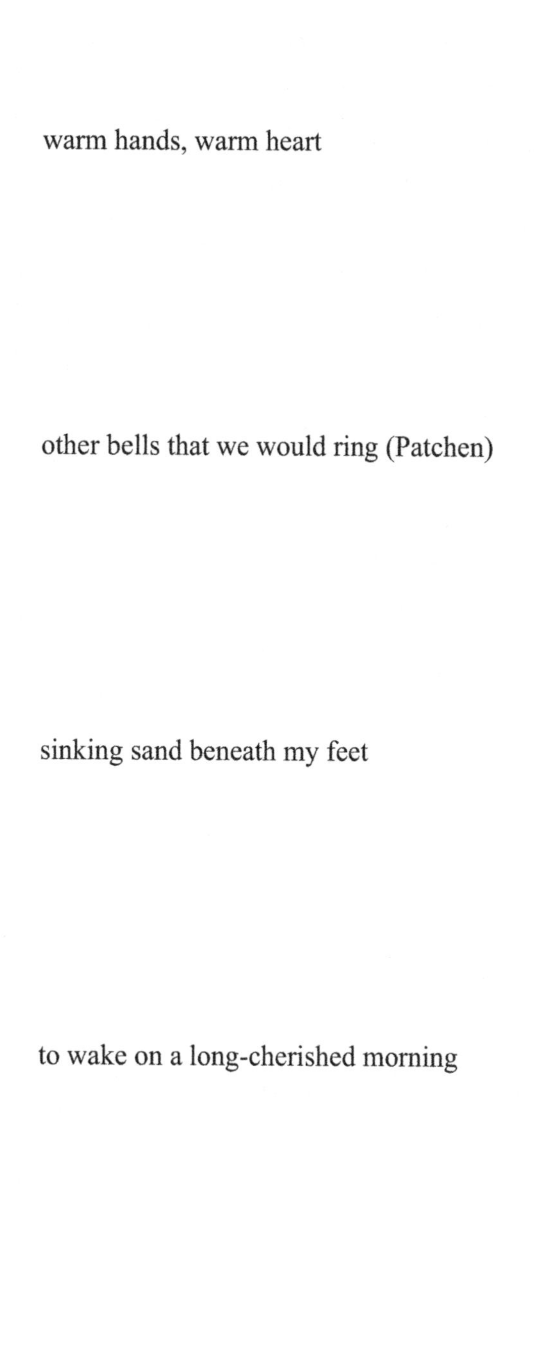

warm hands, warm heart

other bells that we would ring (Patchen)

sinking sand beneath my feet

to wake on a long-cherished morning

digging in the dirt

skipping down the street

"unleash the struggling harmony"
(Davidson)

cooled drips of candle wax

swimming with Kona manta rays

sunlight plays a pivotal role

Language As Power

This section is from a post I wrote for the Insecure Writer's Support Group Blog Hop in May, 2019 as an answer to the following question:

What was an early experience where you learned that language had power?

When I was a young child, I stayed the night at my grandmother's house across the street as often as I possibly could because I loved the way she told stories - fairy tales and stories from her childhood. I loved the ones from her childhood best. Her voice brought every moment to life.

Not all of my friends understood my grandmother, even when I was young. She had been born with a cleft palate and it was fixed via surgery when she was ten - an age when most of our language and speech patterns have become fixed. To me, her voice was beautiful and her words were clear.

As an older child, when I was around the age of ten, my grandmother had a stroke and moved in with us. When we went out to eat together as a family and she ordered her meals, servers often didn't understand her. I was shy and my parents were working on me to speak up, so if a server didn't understand her, it became my job to clarify her order. I learned speaking mannerisms could help or harm a person - words and their presentation have power, even in a simple moment of ordering a meal.

A few months ago, I answered a submission call for a Mother's Day story collection. It's a different kind of collection - a spoken collection with an AI. This means the stories (or, in my case more of an essay) are told in a storytelling style with the voice of an AI. It's a different kind of writing than the usual short story writing. It has a different ebb and flow. It reminds me a little of my grandmother's stories, which is why I wrote my essay "Grandmother's Legacy" for the collection.

Language, both written and spoken, is extremely powerful. It can shape the way we think. It can certainly shape how other people "hear" us or even treat us.

Like in my previous section, I recommend writers answer this question for themselves. What was an early experience, or recent experience, where you learned that language had power?

Knowing your answer will again help you understand your reason “why” you write, which will help you, in turn, keep on writing through the tough moments.

PROMPTS 351-400

rock the boat

to love and let go

swimming to the dock in the middle of the lake

a country girl

a baby’s fingers curling around my own

hiking on loose rocks

walking in the rain

shake it off

a cracked doll's cup

as the crow flies

by the book

a fly on the wall

a bright glow in the dark

red glitter

yet, if they press me

screaming sirens

dusty figurines on a shelf

story time at the library

“fair is foul and foul is fair” (Shakespeare)

old news

a cat with a mustache

a fencing jacket slung over a chair

“close to the sun in lonely lands”
(Tennyson)

I saw myself

no law except the sword

my task is ended

it is not impossible that I will make the catch

hop scotch patterns

living tongues of flame

walking in the moonlight

an octopus attempting to hide in a glass
aquarium

a double-edged sword

a heavy step

the first daffodils of spring

running to slide on ice

a quest

catching crawdads in the creek

catcalls and thrown trash

a cozy of kittens

beware the Ides of March

the camera cannot lie, or can it?

full tilt

poetic justice

light of the world

they shot him down like a dog in the
highway

klaxons sounding

a metal rose

opening a soft envelope

"parting is such sweet sorrow"
(Shakespeare)

write your worries in sand

5 Wise Reasons to Write with Obi Wan Kenobi (and the Star Wars universe)

Before I get into those five reasons, I need to explain why I wrote this section. Years ago, I had an idea to write a series of posts on my blog entitled "Five Reasons to Write" and I invited other authors to take part in the series by coming up with either a "Five Reasons to Write With ____" and they would fill in the blank, or "Five Reasons to Write ____." This spurred a flurry of creative posts and I gained insights into why other writers write and what helps each of us on our creative journey.

I recommend writing your own Five Reasons to Write, Five Reasons to Write _____, and Five Reasons to Write With ___. It can help you know your "why" and help you stay the course for your writing goals. In addition to writing some serious reflections on your writing purpose, I also recommend having some fun with those prompts. Think of a fictional character you enjoy, and think of how this character might inspire your writing. That's what I did with Obi Wan Kenobi here.

Five Reasons to Write with Obi Wan Kenobi.

1. "Be mindful of your thoughts Anakin. They'll betray you."

Be mindful of your thoughts while writing. Don't let your insecurities betray you.

2. "Patience. Use the force. Think."

So, the rough draft just walked into a crowded bar and shape-shifted into something unrecognizable, don't give up. Have patience. Use the writing craft. Think through the problem. (Then, stalk and attack!)

3. "If you spent as much time practicing your saber techniques as you did your wit, you'd rival Master Yoda as a swordsman."

Daydreaming about writing only goes so far. Put pen to paper or hands to keyboard and write!

4. "Mos Eisley spaceport: You will never find a more wretched hive of scum and villainy. We must be cautious."

When confronted with Imperial Storm Troopers of Grammar, the scum of plot issues, and the villainy of harsh critics, don't run away. Just proceed with caution and carry your light-saber silently.

5. "You have taken your first step into a larger world."

Every word takes us on our first steps into a larger world of story writing. Keep it up.

Bonus: "That's no moon. It's a space station."

Write with high stakes!

PROMPTS 401-450

an empty frame

cold feet

“we wear the mask” (Dunbar)

evening prayers

snorkeling with sharks

"ring out, wild bells, to the wild sky"
(Tennyson)

a compass that doesn't point north

planting seeds in the dust

a picnic of pretend princesses

purple stains on a white shirt

loud whispers

the word carved into the bench

the road winds on and on

a pod of orcas leap through a pod of kayaks

thunderstorms persist

a single canoe paddle

a city guy

a lost child

hat trick

rainy day money

those who live in glass houses should not
throw stones

"Believe," she whispered.

the road lay bare in the moonlight

jet engines whining

gentle waters

green pastures

thorns prick the skin

a late-night diner

“there’s daggers in men’s smiles”
(Shakespeare)

the ticking clock

following in his footsteps

a single seagull

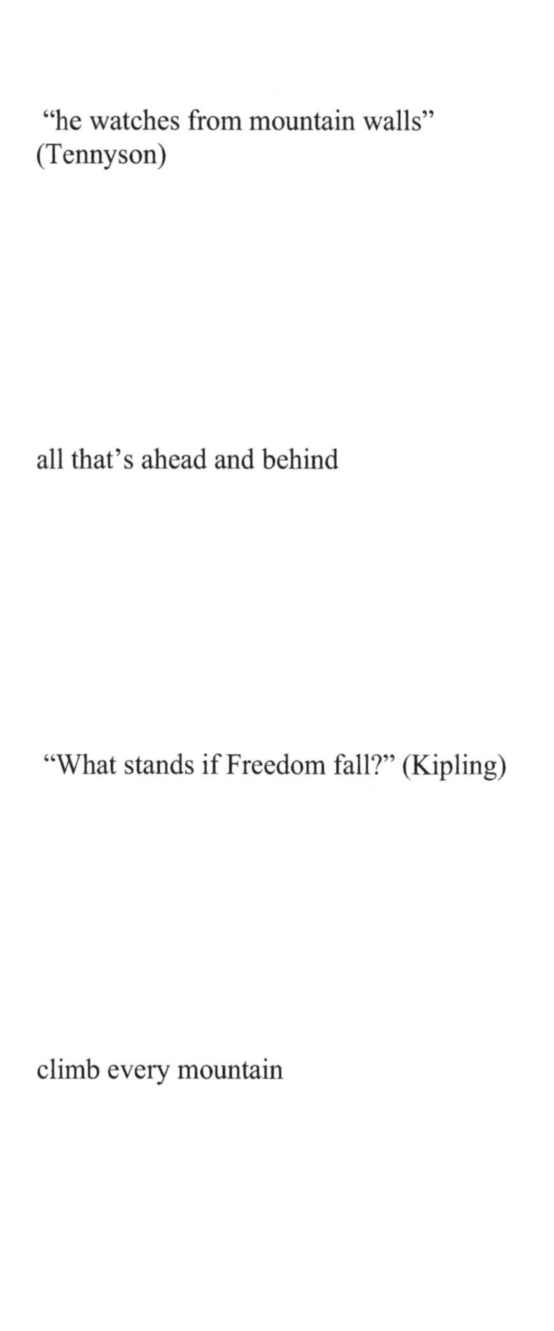

"he watches from mountain walls"
(Tennyson)

all that's ahead and behind

"What stands if Freedom fall?" (Kipling)

climb every mountain

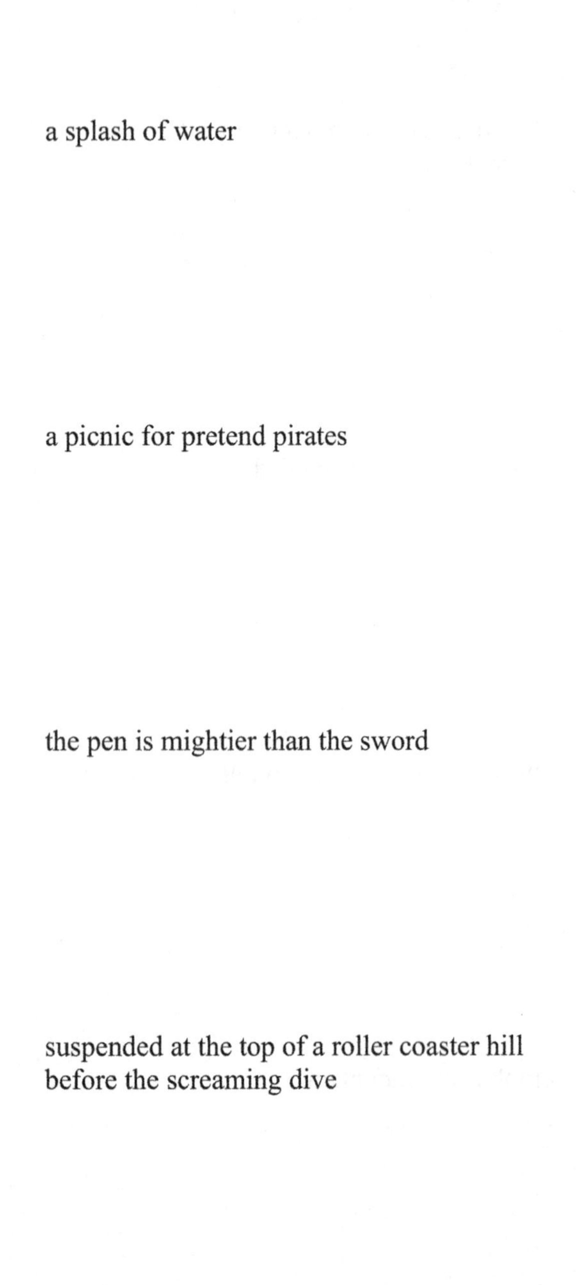

a splash of water

a picnic for pretend pirates

the pen is mightier than the sword

suspended at the top of a roller coaster hill
before the screaming dive

mole hills twist in rhythmic rows

the high plateau above the huge caldera

sweat over strained muscles

a treasure hidden in a field

finding a friend

by hook or by crook

opening a can of worms

the roar of the crowd

salt and pepper

all is locked and barred

5 Reasons to Write Hint Fiction, and 5 More Reasons to Write Drabble and Flash Fiction

This section is a revised version of the original “5 Reasons to Write Hint Fiction” which featured on my blog several years ago. I changed it because I wanted to add a bit about Drabble and Flash Fiction, and why I write a combination of these modern, extremely short forms of story writing.

5 Reasons to Write Hint Fiction:

1. Topping out at 25 words a story, hint fiction is short enough to write on a coffee break.

2. It's fun! I bet you can't write just one.

3. Subject matter is everywhere. Look out the window. Stare at the desk. Glance at a headline. All systems go, and you have a story.

4. It gets me through the daunting days of writing. I can at least write one hint fiction story - even if I don't have time, confidence, or brain-power for anything longer,

5. There are markets for it, and it's a good way to start spreading your author name all over cyberspace.

5 More Reasons to Write Drabble and Flash Fiction.

Drabble Fiction and Flash Fiction are the more "known" styles of extremely short fiction, although rules vary per publisher. Drabbles are 100 words (some places state this must be exact, some are okay with anything under 100 words). Flash Fiction are usually, but not always, 1000 words. Some publishers accepting Flash like only 300 words, some like 500 words, and some like 1500 words. Flash never goes beyond 1500 because anything longer is put in the category of Short Story, which can range between 1600 and 7500 words.

1. Drabble and flash fiction can be written on a lunch break. Any writer pressed for time, struggling with carving out space in their day for writing, or interrupted regularly (small children, a demanding job, or caring for the elderly all involve

necessary interruptions), can find time to write drabble or flash fiction.

2. Drabbles and flash fiction stories are often a great way to explore new ideas or characters. When a writer is in the middle of one, giant work-in-progress (WIP), and feels a yearning to write a new story, a drabble story or a flash fiction story can give the writer a way to explore those new ideas without taking too much time away from the main work on their desk.

3. Short forms of story can give a writer a way to break free and really try new things. If a writer feels stuck in a write with writing the same kind of characters or the same

genre, or the same story theme on repeat, the writer can explore new characters, new genres, or new themes in these short forms. With drabbles and flash fiction stories, I've written characters I never expected to write about: killers, vampire fairies, werewolves, victims of human trafficking. I've also used these short forms to explore different genres and different POV. I think it's important for a writer to continue to push the edge of their abilities and to work to improve their writing craft. Drabbles, flash fiction stories, and other short forms of writing give me the place and freedom to play with words and try new ways of writing.

4. Drabbles and flash fiction stories force a writer to focus in on the

absolute necessities of a story. What needs to be kept? What can be thrown out? Long introductions have no place in drabbles or flash fiction stories. Description needs to fit within a handful of powerful phrases, metaphors, and specific words. Drabbles and flash fiction stories often create a narrow channel for tight writing and this can cause unexpected growth for a writer.

5. Focus is essential in these short forms, which means the purpose of the story needs to shine bright, while not usually given out like a lesson learned at the end of an Aesop's Fable.

If you haven't tried hint, drabble, or flash fiction before, I recommend it. And, if you write something you like, send it out into the world. There are publishers who specialize in each of these short forms.

PROMPTS 451-500

blue sky day

browning bananas on the counter

story time at the lake

teach the torches to burn bright

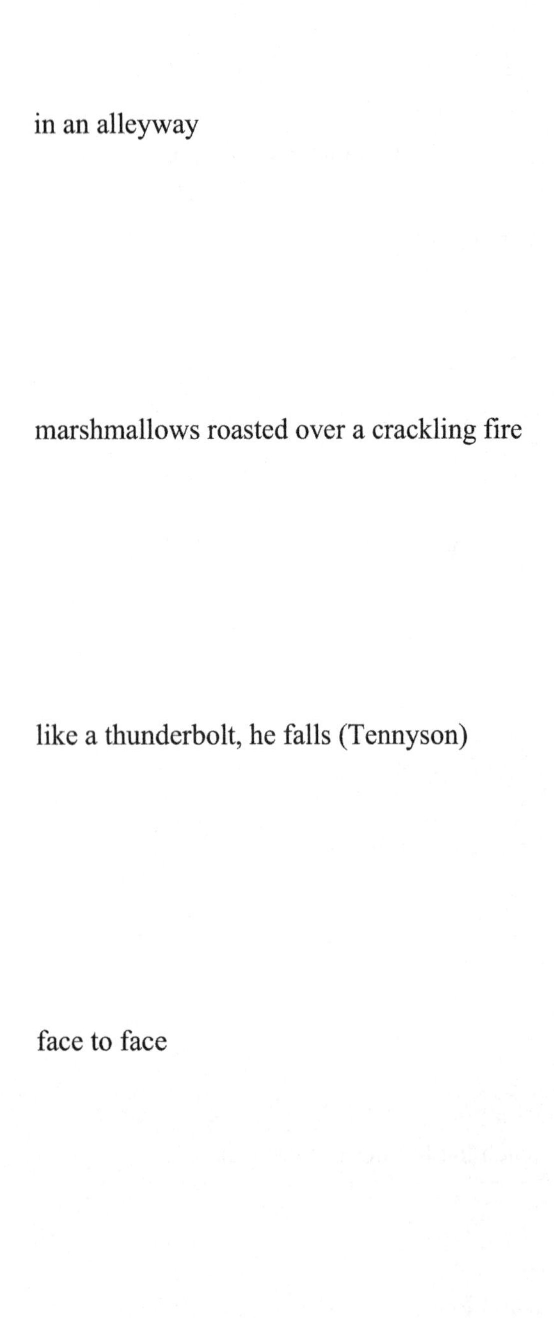

in an alleyway

marshmallows roasted over a crackling fire

like a thunderbolt, he falls (Tennyson)

face to face

iron sacrifice

thirsty suns

blackberry tangles

Dear Dragon,

hands like rawhide

crammed into a tiny plane seat between
passengers

damp aquarium air in a dark basement

looking beyond the inspiring landscapes

a country guy

making an enemy

graveyard shift

keep it under your hat

red sky in the morning, sailor take warning

waterfall

lend me your ears

when the battle’s lost and won

carve your blessings in stone

worn shoes

a deep throw of stars

love and forgetfulness

silent fortitude

many voices sweet

muddy fingers

barefoot in the grass

sullen grace

swaying on the subway

what the dog rolled in

the morning of the wedding

hit the ground running

let your hair down

coffee and tea

a fine day

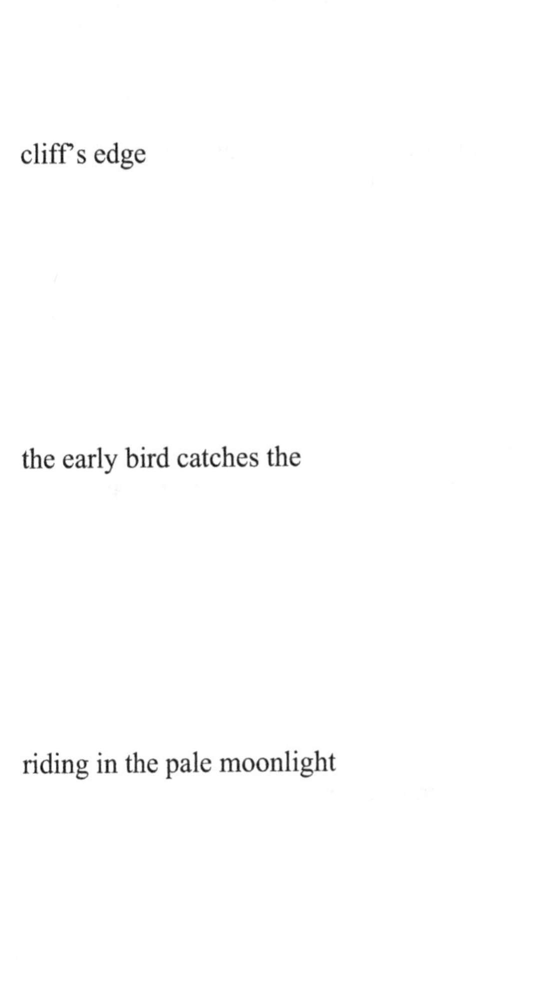

cliff's edge

the early bird catches the

riding in the pale moonlight

sunshine streamed through the blinds

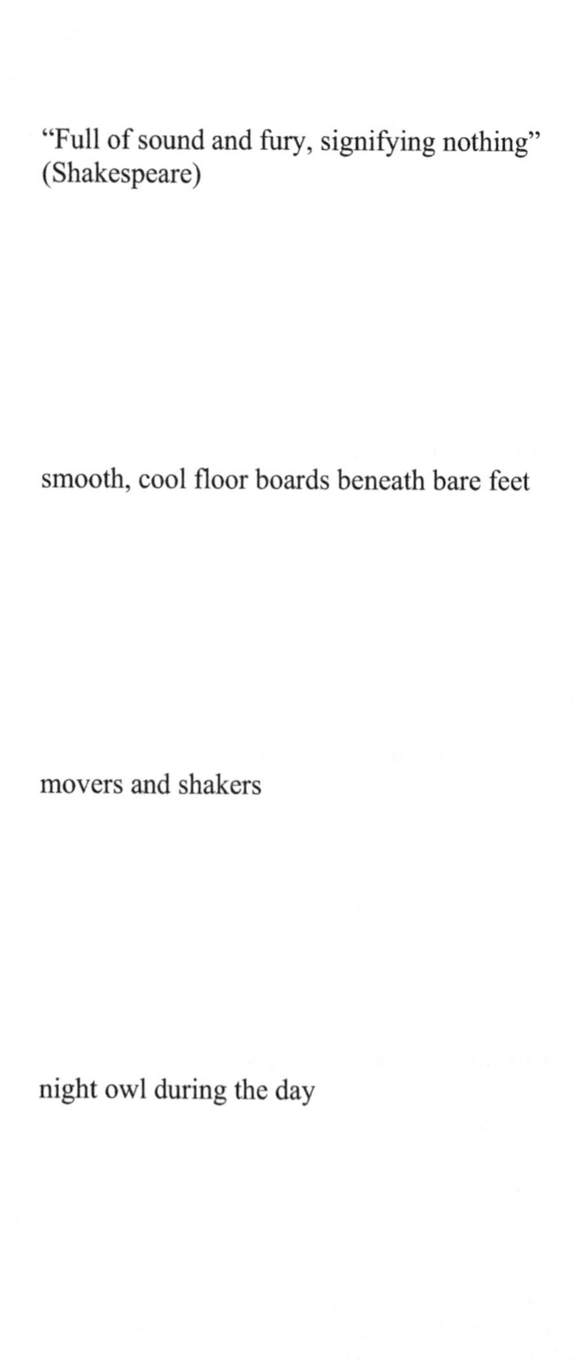

“Full of sound and fury, signifying nothing”
(Shakespeare)

smooth, cool floor boards beneath bare feet

movers and shakers

night owl during the day

once in a blue moon

“plaiting a dark red love knot into her long black hair” (Noyes)

Just Take a Walk

What do you do when you hit a wall with your writing?

You could take a walk. It's a tried and true way to break your mind free of distractions and worries. Look and listen for the unexpected, or just lose yourself in reflection. Don't try to think about your WIP, characterization problems, or that horrid first draft, just walk. Pray, if you pray. Reflect.

Let your feet take you on familiar paths or somewhere new.

Some writers who have walked to free up their writing are: Henry David Thoreau, J.K. Rowling, Earnest Hemingway, Orson Scott Card, C. S. Lewis, and J.R.R. Tolkien.

You never know, maybe a walk in your neighborhood will give you an idea for your character's journeys. As Alan Jacobs states in The Narnian, "…there is a great deal of walking in Narnia: in almost every book some of the characters set off on long journeys by foot ….Likewise, when considered from a certain point of view, The Lord of the Rings is hardly anything but friends going on long – really long – walks together."

So, if you find yourself stalled out in your writing, just take a walk.

PROMPTS 501-547

the rumble boil of water

bucket list

run the gauntlet

jingle bells

sand trickling through my fingers

old habits

Christmas ornaments shining

a stuffy head

crooked hands

a wrinkled sea

a manger

these little birds

before the moment is gone

put the mask on

the wind is rising

my name means it all

hard hearts

hands stained with tree sap

out of sight, out of mind

sand castles

my lips remember

longing to disappear

into your warm embrace

standing on solid rock

roaring with laughter

stretching arms to the sky

the last candle burning low, but bright

the wild purple of the sun

Hell's Canyon

a twisty road

whitewater

river float

avalanche alley

swept away

wildlife canyon

under a smoke-filled sky

nestled in a valley

below the waterfall

into the rapids

underway

a family camper on the side of the road

fishermen

a still pool

a swirling eddy

the remains of a bridge

wading in

sunlight to moonlight

WHERE DO I FIND WRITING PROMPTS?

The answer to that question is: everywhere! The world around us, newspaper titles, song titles, poetry, experiences I've had, and questions I've asked. I highly recommend making a list of writing prompts. Keep a list of phrases that stand out to you, or experiences that you've had. After these simple words and phrases are listed out, jumble them up, let them sit on a shelf for a while, and then bring them out for new use.

About the Author

Tyrean Martinson lives and writes in the Pacific Northwest. An avid daydreamer and reader, Tyrean has studied the art of writing through various book resources and classes. Her first love in genre fiction is fantasy, seconded by sci-fi and most of the variations of those two genres. She also enjoys some contemporary fiction and poetry, with occasional forays into historical and romance fiction.

Writing and the study of writing make up a majority of Tyrean's life, but she also loves to walk, hike, bicycle, and ski or snowboard. She also tutors students from middle school and high school. Tyrean hopes that with each book, story, and poem she writes, she will grow as a writer. She shares her experiences with her students and encourages them to persevere past any kind of rejection, whether it's the kind of rejection in a rejection letter from a magazine editor or any kind of social rejection that teens often face.

Tyrean is currently hard at work on a few novels and a new non-fiction title.

Find Tyrean online at Tyrean's Tales – An Intersection of Faith, Imagination, Encouragement, and Adventure (tyreanstales.com)

WHAT'S NEXT

Keep on writing. Finish a piece. Send out work. Repeat. Editing and revision take place in the finishing bit, but don't overdo these stages. Finish. Send out your work. Start again (even before you hear back about the work you sent out).

If you liked these prompts or this book, reviews are awesome!

You might also be interested in:

5…4…3…2…1…Write!: 25 Speculative Fiction Prompts

OTHER TITLES BY Tyrean Martinson

WORLD OF ARMATIR BOOKS, LISTED IN ORDER OF TIMELINE

Dark Blade: Forged, a currently a Kindle Vella novel, but forthcoming in ebook and paperback

Dark Blade: Tempered (Dark Blade, Vol 2), forthcoming in 2023 as a Kindle Vella series

Champion in the Darkness, The Champion Trilogy Book 1

Champion in Flight, The Champion Trilogy Book 2

Champion's Destiny, The Champion Trilogy Book 3

THE RAYATANA

Liftoff, The Rayatana, Book 1

Nexus, The Rayatana, Book 2

Resonance, The Rayatana Book 3 (Forthcoming, title may change.)

SHORT STORY AND POETRY COLLECTIONS

Light Reflections

Dragonfold and Other Stories/Adventures

Flicker: A Collection of Short Stories and Poetry

25 Impossible Tales of Survivors, Flawed Heroes, and Annoyed Villains

Micro-Multiverse (Forthcoming, title may change)

NON-FICTION TITLES

Summer Vacation Devotions

Walking with Jesus: Stories from One Hope Church (contributor and editor)

A POCKET-SIZED JUMBLE OF 500+ WRITING PROMPTS

Jumble Journal 1

Jumble Journal 2

5…4…3…2…1… WRITE! 25 Speculative Fiction Writing Prompts

Dynamic Writing 1, 2, and 3 (currently out of print)

EXPERIMENTAL FICTION AND SHORT TITLES

Ashes Burn, Seasons 1-7, a Hint Fiction Story

Seedling

The Bridge Snap

When Okay is Enough

WITH BLUE FORGE PRESS

Eight if by Sea, Ghost Sniffers #5

WITH DANCING LEMUR PRESS

"Of Words and Swords" in the 2017 IWSG Anthology Hero Lost: Mysteries of Death and Life

MAJOR RETAILERS WHERE BOOKS ARE SOLD

AMAZON https://www.amazon.com/Tyrean-Martinson/e/B00BCKPHZK/

BARNES AND NOBLE "Tyrean Martinson" | Barnes & Noble® (barnesandnoble.com)

KOBO "TYREAN MARTINSON" | eBook and audiobook search results | Rakuten Kobo

APPLE Tyrean Martinson on Apple Books

MAJOR REVIEW SITES

GOODREADS Books by Tyrean Martinson (Author of Champion in the Darkness) | Goodreads

BOOKBUB Tyrean Martinson Books - BookBub

Made in the USA
Middletown, DE
13 January 2024